SPECTACULAR
STORIES
FOR CURIOUS KIDS
EARLY READER EDITION

Contents

"Don't Shoot, I Have Your Dog!"

During the Revolutionary War, the early American people were fighting to be free from the King of England. These people were known as patriots. One of the main leaders of the patriots was George Washington. You have probably heard of him. He was the first president of the United States.

During the war, the patriots were fighting the British soldiers. The two groups did not like each other. They used sneak attacks to surprise each other during battle.

One night, George Washington thought he had a great plan. A thick fog surrounded the area where the British soldiers were camping. Washington and his troops planned an attack. They thought the fog would help them hide. The fog made it very hard to see. Some of the troops ended up shooting at their own soldiers. This was not a good idea. Washington ordered all his men back to their camp.

As the patriots were going back to camp, they found a little lost dog. The dog had on a fancy collar. The name on the collar read "William Howe." The dog belonged to the leader of the British soldiers!

The patriots took the lost dog to George Washington. They thought the dog could be used for ransom against the other side. They

were surprised by what George
Washington did instead.

George Washington was
an honest man. He also was
a dog lover. He wanted to be
sure that William Howe got his
dog back safely. Washington
ordered a ceasefire. This is an
order for both sides to stop
fighting. While they were waiting
to return the dog, Washington
took good care of the little guy.
He fed him and gave him fresh
water. He brushed all of the
mud out of the dog's coat.

When it was safe, Washington
sent a few of his soldiers to
return the dog. He pinned a
note to the dog's collar. The

note explained what happened. William Howe was very happy to get his dog back.

George Washington did the kind thing by returning the dog. Some people think that Washington wanted to spy on the British camp. Other people think that he was just a good man who really liked animals. What do you think? What would you have done?

Good Guys Break Into Banks Too

The Bank of England holds the second largest collection of gold in the world. It is the repository for approximately 5,600 tons of gold, worth nearly $171 billion! Wow, that place must be incredibly secure. And it is! The walls of the gold vault are nearly

8 feet thick, making it nearly impossible to break into.

The bankers who work at the Bank of England in London take great pride in their institution. The bank has never been robbed or breached by thieves. However, there was one instance when an honest man managed to break into the vault, surprising all the workers with his cleverness.

In 1836, the bank director received a letter from an individual claiming that he could steal as much gold as he wanted from the vault. The director laughed it off, not taking the threat seriously. After all, he believed breaking into the vault was an impossible feat.

A few weeks later, another letter arrived, requesting a meeting with the bank director inside the vault. This posed a significant dilemma—only bank personnel were allowed access to the vault. Nevertheless, the bank director agreed to the meeting, and when the scheduled time arrived, a man emerged through the floor of the vault. Thankfully, he was not a villain.

This man was a worker for the London sewer system. London has an extensive network of tunnels that run beneath the city, some dating back hundreds of years. While inspecting and conducting repairs, he stumbled upon a very old tunnel that led directly under the Bank of England.

A supervillain might have seized the opportunity to steal all the gold, but this sewer worker was a very honest person. He wanted to inform the bank director, ensuring the

safety of the gold. The bank director was very grateful, and together, they sealed off the tunnel, preventing any potential threat. It was a close call! As a token of appreciation, the bankers rewarded the sewer worker with 800 British pounds, equal to $80,000 today.

This story isn't widely known, as it is believed that the bank director preferred not to publicize it. He wished to avoid encouraging others to find ways to breach the bank's security. There was a hint of embarrassment that a sewer worker had managed to accomplish what others couldn't.

The sewer worker could have easily stolen all that gold, but he chose to do the right thing by being honest and helping the bank. He knew that if he had stolen the gold, he might have been caught and sent to jail. As it turned out, he made the right choice and received a generous reward as a result.

A Dangerous Midnight Ride

Have you learned about
Paul Revere? During the
Revolutionary War, Paul was a
hero. He rode his horse through
town late at night. He woke up
the people. He warned them that
the British soldiers were coming.
This gave the people time to get

ready and be safe. His brave ride helped save people's lives. It helped them be ready for battle.

Two years later, another hero made a similar ride. Sybil Ludington was a girl and she was only sixteen years old. She lived with her family on a farm in New York. Her father was a well-known man. The other farmers liked him and trusted him. He was the leader for the army group in that area. It was a group of about four hundred men. The other soldiers were farmers, just like Sybil's dad. They all wanted to be free of British control. They were willing to fight for it if needed.

In the spring of 1777, British ships landed in Connecticut. They had about two thousand soldiers. The soldiers didn't want the townspeople to be free from Great Britain's rules. They began to march to towns. They burned supplies and houses. The townspeople needed help. They needed to warn other towns that British soldiers were coming.

A messenger from the town rode his horse to Sybil's family farm. He told her father what was happening and asked for help. Could this local group of farmer soldiers help? They could! There was just one problem. None of the farmers were there. They all had their own farms and were at home to plant crops for the spring.

Sybil offered to do an important job. Her dad needed to stay at home and make a plan. He needed to prepare. Someone needed to ride to all the other farms and tell the soldiers. This person needed to be brave and smart. Sybil was just the girl for the job!

She got on her horse named

Star. It was a dark, rainy night. Sybil headed out. She rode to all the nearby farms. She carried a stick with her so she could tap on doors and windows. All night long she yelled out, "The British are burning Danbury. Muster at Ludington's at daybreak!" This told the soldiers what was happening and that they were needed to fight. Sybil was alone riding in the dark all night long. She had to be brave and strong.

Sybil returned home as the sun was coming up the next morning. She and Star had ridden forty miles. They had completed their task. All of the soldiers had gathered at the farm. Her dad had a plan. They were ready.

Thanks to Sybil, the soldiers were ready to march. They headed out to help other towns. They managed to help the other towns push the British soldiers out of the area. They protected their farms and families.

Even though she was just a young girl, Sybil knew her father and other people needed her. She chose to be a brave helper. She used her courage to help others. Kids can always help others when they choose to be brave.

Two Orphan Friends who BOTH Became Governors

This is the story of two orphan boys who were down on their luck. They didn't let this keep them down, and they both ended up being very successful adults. Here is their story.

In the late 1800s, America faced a problem. The cities were filled with orphaned children and there was no one to take care of them. An orphan is a child who doesn't have any parents. These children lacked food and a safe place to stay. Often, they had to resort to stealing food. They had to be tough to survive on the streets alone.

This was a big problem. Who could help these children? Some leaders pondered over this issue and devised a plan. Farmers in the Midwest had abundant land and usually enough food. They also needed extra help on their farms. They decided to offer these orphans a chance to take a train to the Midwest, where they could be adopted and finally find safety and families.

Two orphans seized this opportunity. They both boarded the train to Indiana and ended up sitting next to each other, forming a strong

friendship. John Brady was eleven years old and had experienced a difficult life. He got into lots of fights and was so tough that he even had a tattoo! The other boy was Andrew Burke, who had been an orphan since he was four years old.

When they got to Indiana, the boys went their separate ways but remained friends for the rest of their lives. John was adopted by a state senator who believed he was the most unpromising child on the train and wanted to see if he could help him. Andrew, on the other hand, was adopted by a farming family and later became a drummer boy in the Civil War.

The senator who adopted John must have done an excellent job, as John excelled in school and became a hardworking man. He pursued a career as a preacher and moved to Alaska with his wife. Eventually, he became the governor of the state.

After the end of the Civil War, Andrew returned to Indiana. He worked hard, completed his college education, got married, and moved to North Dakota. He worked as a bookkeeper and a banker, and after several years, he was elected as the governor of North Dakota.

These two orphans faced a challenging start in life and experienced some misfortune. However, they decided to change their luck. They took a chance by boarding the orphan train and worked hard to make their lives better. They got an education, learned new skills, and both ended up leading great lives. They had families and had important jobs running an entire state.

Do you ever feel like you're experiencing a streak of bad luck? Is there anything you can do to change it? Sometimes, you have to put in hard work and be open to new opportunities. Don't let a bit of bad luck bring you down!

Weird Jobs

What do you do if you need to get up early for school? You might set an alarm. Or maybe your mom sets an alarm and wakes you up. But what did people do before they had alarm clocks?

Even a long time ago, people had to get up early to go to work. They didn't have any fancy alarm clocks that they could set. They definitely couldn't press the snooze button and try to get a few more minutes of sleep! So how did they know it was time to get up?

In Great Britain, people hired a knocker-upper. *"A WHAT?"* A knocker-upper had a funny name. It was a person who went around knocking on doors at a certain time to wake people up. It was like a living alarm clock!

At first, knocker-uppers would knock on the front door or ring the doorbell. Often, this woke up everyone in the house. Sometimes it even woke up the neighbors. This didn't make them happy.

So knocker-uppers started using long sticks with soft hammers on the end to lightly tap on the window of the person needing to wake up. Sometimes they even used little pea shooters to shoot small pebbles at the window. That sounds fun! The knocker-upper would tap on the window until it opened. This signaled that the person was out of bed. Then the knocker-upper would move on to the next house.

While the job of a knocker-upper sounds fun, they didn't get paid very much. Usually, each person paid their knocker-upper about 12 cents per week. If you had several customers, this could add up. Every little bit helped. What would happen if you didn't pay your knocker-upper? They wouldn't wake you up, and then you would be late for work!

There was even a fun tongue twister kids used to say about knocker-uppers.

We had a knocker-up, and our knocker-up had a knocker-up,
And our knocker-up's knocker up didn't knock our knocker up,
So our knocker-up didn't knock us up, 'Cos he's not up.

Try saying that one fast! That does make me wonder if knocker-uppers had to hire knocker-uppers to wake them up. Thank goodness we have alarm clocks now to do that job for us.

A Running Rebel

Do you like to run? It can be really fun to use your legs to go fast and feel the wind on your face. Rebel Hays loves to run.

He's pretty fast, too. Rebel has even run in high school cross-country races. That's pretty cool because Rebel was only in fourth grade!

How does a fourth-grader get to run in high school races? Rebel is a guide runner. This means he helps to lead one of the students at the high school. This student is blind. Rebel helps him know where to go.

Rebel started running when he was young. For five years in a row, Rebel won his city's Fun Run. One day, Rebel went to pick up his older cousin from running practice. Rebel saw two runners working as guide runners. He thought it was pretty neat. He could do that, too.

The high school coach had seen Rebel run. She knew he

was fast. She knew he had a kind heart. She thought he would be perfect for the job. A guide runner has to be in very good shape. It is harder to be a guide runner than to run your own race. A guide runner has

to be able to run at the same pace as the runner. They have to be able to talk to the runner about any obstacles like turns, ditches, or hills.

Rebel was paired up with Paul Scott. Paul was a tenth grader, and he was blind. Paul liked the idea of running. He felt like it was a nice break from the hard work he did in school. He liked to achieve his goals. But it is hard to run in a race if you are blind.

Paul and Rebel made a great match. To run together, they each hold the end of a three-foot rope. Rebel is fast. He likes to encourage Paul. They started off running two-mile races together. Now they mostly run 5K races. A 5K is 3.1 miles. They are always trying to improve their time and get better.

Rebel says he does get nervous before a race. He always wants to make sure he does his best for Paul. They have become good friends. Rebel likes being able to use his talent to help others. What talents do you have? What can you do to help others and share your talents?

Kids CAN Change the World!

Do you think kids can help change the world? I do! Kids have big ideas and work hard to make the world a better place.

This is the story of Samantha Smith. When Samantha was just ten years old, she had something important on her mind. She decided to take action. Samantha lived during a time when the United States and the Soviet Union were building lots of weapons. These nuclear weapons were very dangerous. It seemed like a war might happen between the two countries.

Samantha lived in the United States. She was worried. She did not want her country to go to war. She knew her friends and neighbors did not want a war. She thought that in the Soviet Union there were kids just like her. They probably didn't want a war either.

Samantha wanted to share her ideas. She wrote a letter to a very important person. This person was the leader of the Soviet Union named Yuri Andropov.

Dear Mr. Andropov,

My name is Samantha Smith. I am 10 years old. Congratulations on your new job. I have been worrying about Russia and the United States getting into a nuclear war. Are you going to vote to have a war or not? If you aren't please tell me how you are going to help to not have a war. This question you do not have to answer, but I would like it if you would. Why do you want to conquer the world or at least our country? God made the world for us to share and take care of. Not to fight over or have one group of people own it all. Please let's do what he wanted and have everybody be happy too.

Samantha Smith

Mr. Andropov was a very busy person. Most people didn't think he would respond to Samantha. But he did!

In his letter, he said that he could tell Samantha was courageous and honest. He told her that his country did not want a war.

He said, "We want peace for ourselves and for all peoples of the planet." Mr. Andropov even invited Samantha and her parents to visit the Soviet Union. He wanted her to see that they

were a peaceful country with nice people.

Samantha and her parents did visit the Soviet Union. Samantha became known as the youngest Goodwill Ambassador. She enjoyed her time learning about the Soviet Union. She met many kind people and made many new friends. She even got to go to camp.

Luckily, war never happened between these two countries. Samantha's honest letter helped both countries understand each other better. She helped people realize that both kids and grownups really just wanted peace.

The First Teddy Bear

Do you have a teddy bear? Lots of kids have teddy bears to play with and love. Do you know where the idea for the first teddy bear started?

The first teddy bear was named after Teddy Roosevelt. Teddy Roosevelt was the president of the United States over one hundred years ago. He is the youngest president in United States history, and he had some new ideas. Many people remember him as the father of the National Parks. He kept over 200 million acres of land for a park system that people still enjoy today.

Do you like to play outside? Mr. Roosevelt loved the outdoors. He liked to hunt, fish, and ride horses. He enjoyed birdwatching. He really liked animals. During his time living in the White House, his family had thirty-two pets! This included normal pets like dogs and cats. It also included a snake, a badger, a pig, and an owl. Mr. Roosevelt and his children loved all their animals.

One day, Mr. Roosevelt was on a bear-hunting trip. It was very cold outside. There weren't any bears to be seen. It seemed like the cold made the bears hibernate early. Mr. Roosevelt and his friends were still enjoying the day.

Mr. Roosevelt got separated from his friends for a little bit. Then he heard them calling out his name. He hurried to find them. He was surprised by what he saw. His friends had found a bear. They had trapped

the bear and tied him to a tree.
They thought Mr. Roosevelt
would shoot the bear. After all,
they were on a bear-hunting
trip. They wanted to make the
president happy.

Mr. Roosevelt did not want to
shoot the trapped bear. He did
not think it was fair. He did not
want to kill a trapped animal.
He told his friends to release the
bear.

This story spread all over the
country. Newspapers everywhere
printed the story. An artist drew
a cartoon of the story. It was
printed in the newspapers. It
showed the president and a cute
bear.

Morris Michtom owned a candy shop. He and his wife also made stuffed animals. They had an idea. They made a cute stuffed bear. They named the bear Teddy's Bear in honor of the president. People loved the stuffed bears and wanted to buy them. The first teddy bear had been created!

The stuffed bears were so popular that the couple ended up making them full time. They sent one to Mr. Roosevelt and his children. Today, kids all over the world own and love teddy bears.

The Royal Truck Mechanic

When you think about queens, you probably think about castles and fancy crowns. You probably do not think about a truck mechanic! But did you know that Queen Elizabeth of England was once a truck mechanic in the British military?

When Elizabeth was a young girl, her father became the King of England. This made her a princess. She lived in the castle and worked hard to learn all of the things she would need to know if she became queen.

When World War II started, Elizabeth knew how important it was to the people of England. She wanted to help and support them. When she turned eighteen, Elizabeth joined the women's branch of the British army. She was the only woman in the royal family to serve in the military.

Elizabeth didn't receive any special treatment even though she was a princess. She had to follow all the same rules as the others. Elizabeth's group was in charge of military vehicles. She learned how to take care of the big army trucks. She could change the oil, top off the fluids, and check the tires. Elizabeth learned how to change tires and rebuild engines. She also learned how to drive! This was a new and exciting thing for a woman during this time, and she loved it. Her friends said that she enjoyed getting dirt under her nails and grease stains on her hands. She saw them as a sign of her hard work and a job well done.

Even though they weren't fighting on the frontlines of the war, the women working on the vehicles still had a dangerous job. Sometimes the trucks were bombed, so the women had to be careful as they drove these big trucks. All of their work was very important to the war efforts.

When the war ended, Elizabeth was very excited. She wanted to celebrate with all the people of England. It was hard being a princess and having so many people recognize you. Elizabeth put on her military uniform. With

her parents' permission, she went out into town. Wearing her military uniform, she looked just like all the other girl soldiers. She was able to celebrate victory with her friends.

Elizabeth eventually became the Queen of England. The people liked Queen Elizabeth. She was always working to help the people of England, just like when she was a young girl joining the military. Queen Elizabeth looked out for the needs of the people and had pride in her country. It's important to help people, even if it means getting your hands a little dirty!

Never Give Up (A Gold Mining Story)

Has anybody ever told you to make lemonade out of lemons? No, they don't mean actual lemonade. This is an expression that means making the best out of something. Sometimes in life, things don't go as planned. When this happens, we can't give up. We have to keep working to make the best of things.

R.U. Darby was just a boy when his uncle had a crazy idea. He wanted to dig for gold out west. Darby headed west with his uncle. They bought some land and the tools needed to dig and mine for gold. They started digging. It didn't take too long before they found gold! They thought they were going to be rich.

They started digging, but then a funny thing happened. They were able to dig up a little gold, but then the area was dry. There was no more gold. Darby and his uncle dug all around but couldn't find any more gold. They were sad and discouraged. They decided to quit.

Darby's uncle sold the land. The new landowner thought there might still be gold there. He hired an expert miner to help. The expert studied the area. He said that gold had probably shifted about three feet over. Sure enough, when the new owner started digging, he found a huge amount of gold. It was only three feet from where Darby and his uncle had given up hope. The new owner made a lot of money from the gold.

Darby learned an important lesson from that experience. He learned that you can't give up when things get hard. Darby kept this lesson with him as he got older. When he got a job, he thought about this. He wanted to always do his best and never give up.

Darby started selling insurance. Sometimes it was hard to make sales. Instead of quitting, Darby worked harder.

He earned people's trust. He started to sell a lot of insurance. Darby became one of the richest insurance salesmen of his time.

Have you ever had a time when things didn't go as planned? Did you ever have a task that just seemed too hard to finish? What did you do? We can learn an important lesson from Darby and never give up. Work hard to go after the things that are important to you. Great things happen for people who work hard!

How Did THAT Seem like a Good Idea?

Annie Taylor was a bit of a daredevil. This means she liked to do things that many people thought were risky. Annie wasn't always this way. She was a hard worker. When Annie was younger, she was a schoolteacher. She also taught music and dance lessons.

As Annie got older, she wanted to be famous. She felt that if she was famous, she could make a lot of money. Annie decided to do something no one else had done before. She wanted to see if she could ride over Niagara Falls in a barrel.

Niagara Falls is a huge waterfall. It is so big it is considered the eighth wonder of the world. It is one of the most powerful waterfalls in the whole world. It drops 160 feet from the top to the bottom. Over six million cubic feet of water flow

over Niagara Falls every minute. Wow! That is a lot of water.

Annie had a special barrel made just for her trip. It was made of oak and iron, so it would be very strong. The inside was lined with a mattress. This would provide padding. The trip over the falls would be very bumpy. No one had ever survived going over Niagara Falls. Would Annie be the first?

Annie wanted to do a test run with the barrel before she tried it herself. She put her pet cat in the barrel and sent it over the falls. Poor kitty! Luckily, the cat survived and only had a few small cuts. This made Annie more confident. She believed it could be done.

A few days later was Annie's 63rd birthday. It was October 24, 1901. It seemed like a great day for a trip over Niagara Falls. At the top of the waterfall, Annie climbed into her barrel. She took her lucky heart-shaped pillow with her. Her friend secured the lid and set the barrel to float in the river. It got swept in the current of the river. In no time at all, the barrel was crashing down Niagara Falls.

A rescue team waited at the bottom of the waterfall. Did Annie survive? They pulled the barrel to shore. They unscrewed the lid. There was Annie, who was alive and only had a small cut on her forehead.

Did Annie enjoy her trip over the waterfall? No! She did not. Annie said she would rather walk in front of a loaded cannon than make another trip down the falls. She recommended that nobody else try it. Annie didn't even become as rich and famous as she had hoped.

Since that day, nearly 125 years have passed. Only sixteen people can claim they have survived going over Niagara Falls. More than five thousand people have died trying. The moral of the story is: Don't try to go over Niagara Falls! Trying to be famous isn't all it's cracked up to be.

Mmm, Mold Juice!

One of the most important discoveries for the world of medicine happened because of a messy room!

Alexander Fleming was a smart guy and a good student. He loved science and worked hard to do well in school. He had a teacher who studied bacteria and invented vaccines.

Alexander thought this was really neat. He wanted to study this as well. He liked using science to help people.

During World War I, Alexander worked in a military hospital. Men were dying during the war. They were also dying in the hospital. They would get infections and get really sick. Doctors didn't have the right medicine to help heal wounds and stop infections. It didn't exist yet! But that was all about to change.

After the war, Alexander went back to London. He was a very smart doctor and a scientist, but his office was a mess! He spent many years making new medicines to help people. He worked with mold and bacteria to do this. He had experiments all over his office.

One summer, Alexander left his office in London. He went on vacation with his family. When he returned, he noticed something weird in one of his experiments. A petri dish was covered in mold. It probably looked very gross. This was normal for Alexander's office.

What was not normal was that in the middle of all that mold was an area that was clean. Hmmm... Alexander's smart mind went to work.

He thought that fungus spores from the office below somehow got into his office. The fungus spores mixed with his mold project. The result would change medicine forever. Alexander realized that this new clue might help treat infections in humans.

At first, he called the medicine "mold juice." Yuck! He used it to treat friends when they were sick. It worked! But here is something crazy. Many other doctors at the time didn't think this new medicine was any good. Poor Alexander still believed in it. He didn't give up. He continued to make the medicine and treated people. He began to call the medicine penicillin.

It would take almost sixteen years for other doctors to realize that penicillin really worked. Thank goodness Alexander didn't give up. Today, penicillin is one of the medicines most used by doctors. It is used to treat all kinds of infections in humans. Have you ever had strep throat or an ear infection? The doctor might have given you penicillin to make you feel better.

Penicillin has saved millions of lives and helped many people feel better. It is all thanks to Alexander Fleming believing in his experiment and not giving up. I guess this is one case where having a messy room turned out to be a good thing!

Mary Sells Sea Shells

Have you ever tried the tongue twister, "Sally sells sea shells by the sea shore"? Did you know this tongue twister was actually written about a real person?

Her name wasn't Sally. It was Mary, but that doesn't quite work with the tongue twister.

Mary Anning lived in England in the early 1800s. Her father loved to search for and collect fossils. He passed his love on to Mary and her brother.

The three of them would spend hours searching the beach and areas around it, looking for interesting shells and fossils. Her father taught them how to identify fossils and collect them without causing damage. Sometimes they would sell the fossils to tourists visiting the beach.

Mary's father died when she was eleven years old. The family was poor and struggled to afford the things they needed. Mary wanted to help her family. She remembered selling fossils with her dad and thought maybe this could help them earn money. She set up a little shop and continued to dig for fossils.

When Mary was only twelve years old, she found an entire skeleton fossil. It was the first complete Ichthyosaurus skeleton of its kind, estimated to be over 200 million years old!

Mary didn't get a formal school education, but she was very smart. She was also skilled at drawing the fossils she found. People would visit her shop to buy her fossils and her drawings of fossils. Her shop became very popular, attracting scientists and museum owners who wanted to see Mary's discoveries. Even famous noblemen purchased fossils for their collections. Mary was happy to be pursuing her passion. She was one of the greatest fossil finders of her time.

Unfortunately, some researchers didn't support Mary because she was a girl. They didn't think that girls could do such remarkable work or make important fossil discoveries. Some scientists even stole her work and claimed it as their own.

Now, over 200 years later, scientists recognize the important contributions Mary made all those years ago. She helped find and identify lots of early fossils. She was just a girl trying to support her family by doing what she loved.

Flying Sausages

Sometimes history has stories that seem a little gross. This is one of those stories. What do sausages and war blimps have in common? You are about to find out!

The German people have always loved sausages. The seasoned meat is stuffed into a small casing. Sausages are full of flavor and are a popular German food. The casings were usually made out of cow intestines. While this might seem gross, the cow intestines were stretchy and could be tightly sealed. This made them the perfect casing for sausages.

But how does this have anything to do with blimps? During World War I, the Germans began using large blimps called zeppelins. These were like giant floating balloons that could fly through the air. Some zeppelins were 800 feet long. That's bigger than two football fields!

The zeppelins weren't very fast. They were used to drop bombs or carry supplies. Their size made them very intimidating to their enemies. Wouldn't you be scared if a giant warship came floating over your house?

The first zeppelins were made of rubber. But there was a problem with that. Rubber was heavy and didn't fly very well. So someone came up with a very smart and weird idea. "Why don't we make them from guts?"

It turns out that the same material used for creating yummy sausages was also perfect for making a zeppelin.

Cow intestines could be stretched and sewn together. They didn't develop holes easily, which was important for the zeppelin to be able to fly. And they were easy to get.

As the Germans began making more zeppelins, they

realized how many cow intestines it was going to take. Each zeppelin used around 250,000 cow intestines. Yuck! That's a lot of guts. The Germans began to get worried. Did they have enough cow intestines to make all the zeppelins they had planned?

The German government put a ban on using cow intestines for anything other than making zeppelins. This meant no more sausages. It was a sad time for sausage lovers everywhere. The government was very serious about this. If you were caught making sausage, you could go to jail.

Luckily, the end of the war brought an end to the building of zeppelins and the ban on sausage making. The German people could go back to making and eating their sausages in peace. I think the lesson here is that sometimes we have to use our imaginations to solve problems.

How Smart Are You? Let's Measure?

A long time ago, do you know how they measured how smart someone was? They looked at the size of their head!

If a person had a big head, then they probably had a big brain inside it. That big brain probably made them really

smart. So, a long time ago,
people with big heads were
thought to be super smart.
People with little heads weren't
quite so lucky.

Who had smaller heads that
were still very smart? Kids
can be very smart, but they
still have small heads. Women
sometimes have smaller heads
than men, but they are still very
smart. Alice Lee didn't think
head size was a good way to tell
how smart someone might be.
She wanted to prove this theory
was wrong.

Alice was a really smart young
woman. She lived in a time
when it was rare for a woman

to go to college. Some men at the time didn't want women to attend college with them. So they used the "big head" theory to prove that they were smarter than women. Alice wanted to change this!

How were brains and skulls measured? Usually, they were measured after a person was already dead. This wasn't much help. Alice really liked math. She was clever. She came up with a way to measure the size of a person's head while they were still alive. A group of men offered to have their heads measured. They probably thought this would prove that men were smarter than women. Boy, were they wrong!

Alice took her measurements. She did the math. The results shocked everyone. Some of the men who were considered the smartest had very small heads. One man, who Alice said was

one of the smartest she'd ever met, had the very smallest head!

Alice tried her study on a different group. This group had both men and women in it. The results were the same. There didn't seem to be any link between head size and how smart a person was. In fact, some women had heads that were bigger than those of really smart men. These men had to admit that they were wrong about head size. Or they had to admit that the women were smarter than they were. What do you think they chose?

Thanks to Alice, scientists now know that head size doesn't

affect how smart you are. Alice had to work hard when many people didn't believe in her. She had to fight to prove that she was right. It's important to stand up for what you believe in. Kids prove every day that they are super smart even though they have small heads!

You Scratch My Back, I'll Scratch Yours

Have you ever heard of a symbiotic relationship? This is when two different animals or people help each other. It is important to have help and support. We have our families and friends to help us out.

What about animals and other creatures?

Just like our family and friends make life better for us, sometimes animals rely on other species to help them. Some of the species helping each other may seem like unlikely pairs. If you look closely, you can see how these strange bonds can benefit both species.

The Nile crocodile is one of the largest reptiles in the world. It can be 16 feet long and weigh 500 pounds. Wow! I bet it has some giant teeth. I don't think I'd want to run into it during a swim. This crocodile lives in Africa. It mostly eats fish, but it will attack anything, even zebras or hippos. The Nile crocodile probably doesn't have many friends. Yet, there is one small creature it gets along with really well.

The small Egyptian Plover is a bird that is only seven inches tall. When the Nile crocodile is lounging next to a river, it will open its mouth wide. The Egyptian Plover will fly right into the giant mouth! The bird picks at the crocodile's teeth. It cleans up any leftover food bits from between the teeth, kind of like dental floss. The bird gets a free meal. The crocodile gets its teeth cleaned. When the bird is done, it simply flies away. What a funny pair!

Here is another pair of African animal friends. The warthog is a tough, sturdy animal. It has razor-sharp tusks that it uses to defend itself. The mongoose is a small, furry critter. When a warthog sees a pack of mongooses, it will lie down. This invites the mongooses over to it. The small, fuzzy mongooses will give the warthog a massage! They will pick up and eat all the ticks and bugs in the warthog's coat. The mongooses get an easy dinner. The warthog gets a nice, clean coat that is free of ticks. That sounds good for both animals.

Our last example of symbiotic relationships comes from the rainforest. Most frogs in the rainforest have to be careful. They are usually food for the giant snakes and spiders that lurk in the trees. There is one tiny frog that isn't too worried about it. Its roommate is the mighty tarantula spider! The microhylid frog is just barely

one inch long. It would be an easy, tasty snack. But it lives with the tarantula spider, the biggest spider in the world! How does this work? The frog eats any insects that might try to eat the tarantula's eggs. In return, the frog gets to sleep peacefully, knowing its giant spider roommate is nearby. I don't think I would sleep peacefully if I had a tarantula for a roommate!

These animals show us how important it is to have others around to help you. Life is easier when you have friends that you can count on. Do you have someone special in your

life who makes you feel safe?
What can you do to be a helper
for someone else?

YOUR REVIEW

What if I told you that just one minute out of your life could bring joy and jubilation to everyone working at a kids book company?

What am I yapping about? I'm talking about leaving this book a review.

I promise you, we take them **VERY seriously**. Don't believe me?

Each time right after someone just like you leaves this book a review, a little siren goes off right here in our office. And when it does we all pump our fists with pure happiness.

A disco ball pops out of the ceiling, flashing lights come on... it's party time!

Roger, our marketing guy, always and I mean always, starts flossing like a crazy person and keeps it up for awhile. He's pretty good at it. (It's a silly dance he does, not cleaning his teeth)

Sarah, our office manager, runs outside and gives everyone up and down the street high fives. She's always out of breath when she comes back but it's worth it!

Our editors work up in the loft and when they hear the review siren, they all jump into the swirly slide and ride down into a giant pit of marshmallows where they roll around and make marshmallow angels. (It's a little weird, but tons of fun)

So reviews are a pretty big deal for us.

It means a lot and helps others just like you who also might enjoy this book, find it too.

You're the best!
From all of us goofballs at Big Dreams Kids Books

Made in the USA
Middletown, DE
02 February 2024